HIDDEN IN
PLAIN SIGHT

HIDDEN IN PLAIN SIGHT

A MEMOIR OF ILLUMINATED BLESSINGS

BY

DARLENE HARTING

Darlene

www.bookstandpublishing.com

Published by
Bookstand Publishing
Morgan Hill, CA 95037
4722_5

ISBN 978-1-63498-849-0

PREFACE

A Christian friend in the midst of an extended hardship once shared she did not know *what* tomorrow held…, but knew *Who* held her tomorrows. Such wisdom contained in so few words! The phrase serves as an intermittent reminder that I will never be alone either, no matter what lies ahead. Ten years ago, this truth resonated when cancer burst a longstanding normalcy bubble. An accustomed-to mountaintop view was instantly obscured, leaving an unfamiliar and alarming valley once the dust settled.

Without delay, God's omnipresence substantially revealed itself in ways that were not always noticed while all was going well. The God on the mountain *is* the very same God Who is in the valley, yet recognition and awe of Him dimmed while favorable steadiness was the norm for five decades. Awareness of His provision, presence, and counsel in the day-to-day continuum was inadvertently being muffled by innumerable worldly distractions: the familiar adage of not being able to see the forest for the trees.

Documenting the journey, although belated, revisits the unsettling period and reminds that things could have turned out quite differently: the gifts of restored health and additional time on earth are miracles.

> *"God whispers to us in our pleasures, speaks*
> *in our conscience, but shouts in our pains.*
> *It is His megaphone to rouse a deaf world."*
> *– C.S. Lewis –*

DEDICATION

Hidden in Plain Sight is dedicated to my husband, Mike, whose unwavering support of this authoring endeavor helped make it possible.

INTRODUCTION — WHY WRITE?

Spring and summer of 2009 found me rocked to the core with an abrupt discovery of eye cancer. Fundamental topics came to light during the thought-provoking ordeal, igniting a desire to pass them along through authorship. Nevertheless, a lack of publishing know-how, time constraints, and insecurities about possible judgmental reactions regularly sidetracked the inexplicable prompting to share the account.

Who am I to contribute any viewpoints about a cancer wake-up call to a reading audience? After all, the health juncture was modest, in light of cancer's reputation for extensive destruction. All the same, the brief chapter still amassed an operative collection of teachable moments, having had sufficient bearing to cause absolute imbalance. The unexpected disruption seized negative attention, while illuminating blessings in tandem: a conceivable theme for a book.

A variety of happenings could stimulate an individual to examine if they are being a good steward with their limited time on earth. An isolated health crisis, though now a decade ago, was the catalyst that stirred an assessment of *my finite stay*. The effort to convey thoughts in writing is not a presumption of self-importance in any way. It has simply been indelibly put on my heart to try, for whatever it may be worth.

Any medical references mentioned are broad, but integral to the account. Spiritual positions and questions surfaced while facing an actuality that appeared bleak. *The entire account is subjective*, but readers may find some themes relatable. The priceless gift of.a stable upbringing has been a mainstay while navigating life, so my deceased parents' and grandparents' influential legacies are deservedly noted.

Hidden in Plain Sight is a vicarious wake-up call, and a testimony of God's provision.

"Publish his glorious deeds among the nations. Tell everyone about the amazing things He does."
– Psalms 96:3 NLT –

TABLE OF CONTENTS

PART I

FIVE DECADES
ON
THE MOUNTAIN

Darlene Harting

1

A Helpful Encounter

At times, paths have crossed with an individual and assistance has materialized in such a specific way that mere 'coincidence' seemed an implausible explanation. Such was the case when introduced to Jeff by a mutual friend returning a section of my sluggishly progressing book draft. Jeff mentioned he was working on a writing project himself, and agreed to critique a small sample. Thus far, three years and umpteen hours had already been invested toward what was an increasingly elusive authoring effort, so soliciting a few random opinions seemed logical. He only read ten minutes worth, yet immediately zeroed in on an integral missing angle. His tactful feedback and constructive insight pointed in an uncharted direction, temporarily restored waning momentum, and directly influenced this opening chapter.

You see, the original plan was to delve right in and reflect on a brief personal bout with cancer. But, it took a stranger to point out that he did not know anything about me, nor would potential readers, *unless they were told*. Was mine a background of wealth or poverty, chaos or stability, good health or chronic ailments, faith or disbelief, city bustle or rural tranquility? He suggested exploring different pivotal life experiences that influenced and molded who I was long before the medical predicament. Up until that time, the narrative was being approached solely from a current middle-aged perspective. Any introductions to an unfamiliar reading audience by canvassing way back in the past had never been considered before.

Yet, summarizing the building blocks key to character development proved to be no easy task. Sifting through a multitude of memories, sorting them sequentially, and specifically trying to convey *their extent* in written form was a tall order. A variegated tapestry of seamless provision was striking as a time line came to life on paper.

Regrettably, neither my parents nor grandparents are alive to see their operative legacies permanently documented. In hindsight, appreciation could have been expressed to all of them more often, when unlimited golden opportunities to do so were still readily available.

Adding elements about growing up to this account can be attributed to the chance encounter with a helpful and insightful stranger.

"Sometimes the greatest adventure
is simply a conversation."
– Amadeus Wolfe –

2

A Firm Foundation

*S*table is the adjective that repeatedly came to mind when searching for a single descriptive word to sum up the overall rhythm from birth to age fifty. That being said, the stability was, and continues to be, *providential and unmerited*. Poverty, abuse, rejection, and other potential burdens, *that could easily riddle one's biography*, miraculously never came to pass.

My parents were born and raised in small Pennsylvania towns about an hour apart. Their first encounter was at a nearby hospital where mom worked as a registered nurse. Dating led to marriage, and after their firstborn arrived they purchased a home on a newly developed street in suburban Ohio. It was a safe middle class area where adults were cordial, neighbors looked out for each other, and there were plenty of kids around: an opportune setup for what would be a growing family.

Dad was a hard working provider and engaged father. An appealing mischievous quality dotted his otherwise low-keyed personality, and he got a real kick out of playing occasional random practical jokes. Mom complimented him with her even-tempered and confident parenting style. The fulfillment she exuded working part-time cardiac nursing positions would eventually inspire five of her seven children to seek careers in health care. She did not waste valuable time and energy nitpicking and obsessing about her superficial outer packaging or that of others. Rather, attention and resources gravitated toward managing responsibilities and pursuing hobbies. All the same, there was a unique self-assurance about the way she carried herself: An analytical problem solver, with a knack for sizing up situations and prioritizing without unnecessary drama. The realization she was quite a tough act to follow would gradually unfold during young adulthood, while attempting to emulate her sureness and level-headed approach to life.

While growing up, my repetitive exposure to infants and toddlers yielded an affinity for them. Second in line to an older sister, I was just days away from turning one when a baby brother was born. Following his arrival, mom would go on to deliver four additional siblings within an eleven year span, so there was oftentimes a little one in the house to dote on and oversee. Age-appropriate responsibilities were handed out by my mom and dad starting when we were young. Being raised alongside three sisters and three brothers made for a well-rounded and unburdened childhood that left many good memories in its wake.

In addition, several of dad's eleven siblings had large families of their own, and mom had one sister as well. The implicit value of extended family was stressed from the get-go by way of steady socializing with a broad medley of aunts, uncles, and cousins; each adding a slice of history, personality, and depth to the family tree.

Sharing the ups and downs of life with six siblings kept us connected, even as we all grew up, moved out, and scattered in different directions. A sister or brother was usually available, but more importantly, receptive, when seeking to either mull over a problem or relish an accomplishment. With maturity came enhanced awareness that familial dysfunction permeated every layer of society, still my comprehension and appreciation of our abiding cohesiveness wasn't fully realized.

"Remember, remember, this is now, and now and now. Live it, feel it, cling to it. I want to become acutely aware of all I've taken for granted."
– Sylvia Plath –

Darlene Harting

3

Glenny: A Pint-sized Champion

Glenny was twelve years younger than me, and the last born of seven children. He was the baby of the family, and we all did what we could to ease his struggles with a congenital illness. A serious liver abnormality was surgically revealed at the tender age of three months, with doctors predicting a dismal two year life expectancy. However, God had a beautiful contrary plan which slowly revealed itself as the two years stretched to *almost eight!*

A courageous little boy, he did not complain about medications, discomfort, or physical limitations: a real trooper and pervasive inspiration during his abbreviated life. His bloated belly, jaundiced skin coloring, and sticklike extremities prompted second looks and oftentimes abrasive staring. Witnessing the gawking hurt terribly, and the goal was always to distract and protect him so *he* wouldn't notice.

With dad and the older children trying to hold things together on our home front, mom stayed by Glenny's side during every hospitalization, some of them dragging on for months at a time. Occasionally, his health decline plateaued providing relative stableness. Those rare respite intervals enabled him to attend elementary school, where he was well loved by classmates and staff.

My parents purchased a lot and trailer at a nearby campground an hour from home, so during the summers he could be a little camper when able. Their smart strategy created an intermittent fun family diversion, while still providing security with the hospital and liver specialists nearby.

Radiating innocence, *and spunk*, he charmed those he met. There was no way to prepare for the profound void following his premature passing two months before his eighth birthday. Having to move on with little Glenny no longer physically there to comfort, care for, and play with was so very hard, but his courageous imprint was permanent.

Being the big sister of a pint-sized champion was a treasured but fleeting privilege that will be forever cherished.

"There are no goodbyes for us. Wherever you are, you will always be in my heart."
– Mahatma Gandhi –

4

What a Great Time to be a Kid

Kids in general spent a good deal of time playing outdoors while growing up in the sixties and seventies. A buffet of advanced technological devices weren't readily available yet in those days to lure children indoors for hours of sedentary isolated amusement. Unstructured outdoor play was popular, and there was oftentimes a pick-up game of some sort with several kids in progress. My siblings, friends, and I moved freely around to these games, the pool, the woods, the drug store, the park, each other's homes etc.

We did not usually venture too far from our general neighborhood, even so, mom was not normally kept abreast of our itineraries and fluctuating whereabouts. It was a different time back then, but unfortunately that type of carefree play is not as prevalent in today's increasingly structured, *and precarious*, world. Looking back, it was a great time to be a kid, and miraculous that we all returned home safely every evening.

Orchestrating rudimentary bake sales and carnivals, as well as role-playing house, school, and television game shows stoked our imaginations. Other popular draws were the city pool, berry picking in the woods, and wintertime sled riding and ice skating at the golf course directly behind our backyard. Boredom was a rare dilemma.

Darlene Harting

"For in every adult there dwells the child that was,
and in every child there lies the adult that will be."
— John Connolly —

5

Solid Examples and Boundaries

Even though Mom and Dad did not parent in a hovering overprotective manner, they surely called for cooperation and obedience. Defiance or disrespect simply wasn't tolerated, and chores came before play; the guidelines consistently uncomplicated. They commanded respect without having to verbalize it very often, but they were also respect*ful*.

Materialistic or covetous parental behaviors were rarely observed. Raising seven children, one of them terminally ill, likely left little time and energy for comparing resources, acquisitions, and entertainment choices with those of peers. In any event, they seemed content with what they had, unconcerned about keeping up with other people or fads, and comfortable in their own skins.

Mom was proficient at stretching groceries, and hand-me-down clothes were routinely utilized. Dad's factory went on strike a couple of times which necessitated food stamps, but they confidently carried on through any lean times without dwelling on the tight finances. The accumulation of possessions was routinely understated, and that learned orientation remained an anchoring point of reference once an adult struggling to manage on my own. It helped neutralize a share of the incessant media messages promoting the falsehood that buying and securing more possessions guaranteed contentment.

Both parents exemplified a sound work ethic, and taught that consequences were inevitable; to prepare for the fallout when making poor choices. The concepts of personal empowerment and accountability came to light in a very real way, because of their sensible tactics. Desired perks and possessions were earned rather than just handed over, and discipline was dispensed fairly. They seemed more concerned with being my parents, not my friends. Rules and boundaries they established created a basic framework for appropriate behavior, providing a safety net and sense of being grounded.

Being put on a pedestal or spoiled with preferential treatment, under the pretense that the world revolved around my needs and wants, would have only been a source of impairment in the long run. It would likely be far more stressful to weather grownup realities if instilled with an exaggerated sense of entitlement as a child or teenager.

The commonsense framework they established set a solid baseline for functioning in society; making it easier to enter jobs and relationships with realistic expectations, all the while facilitating the desired transition to independence.

A sound upbringing and proper nurturing were blessings on every conceivable level.

"The greatest gifts you can give your children are the roots of responsibility and the wings of independence."
— Denis Waitley —

6

Influential Grandparents

A maternal and paternal set of grandparents were central figures, even though a seven-hour round trip drive to their homes hindered frequent visitation. They lived just an hour from each other, so our family spent some time at both homes when the trips to Pennsylvania were made. Children reap abundant benefits from grandparent relationships, yet a wide array of circumstances, both avoidable and unavoidable, could interfere with that bond. Unfortunately, the relationship's worth and influence might even be underestimated or undermined. Sadly, Grandparents sometimes pass away before their grandchildren are even born, or when they are very young. In any case, the opportunity to meet and get to know all four of them well, while sustaining crystal clear memories, is remarkable for sure.

Each one embraced their weighty role, reinforced a sense of security and belonging, and exuded life lessons. Biannual visits to see them were highly anticipated, as evidenced by a carload of impatient kids chanting..."We're almost to our Grandma's hooray, hooray!" toward the end of the boring three and a half hour car ride. Plentiful mid-day meals, a porch swing, the *dreaded* outhouse, and leisurely group walks to the local penny candy store with Grandpap are a few of many fond flashbacks. Observing genuine mutual caring and respect between parents and grandparents showed them making the most of the limited time they were able to spend together.

Years later, when I was a thirty-two year old mom with two young children, there was an unexpected need (and opportunity) to give back in a sense to one Grandma. Mom was very ill at the time, and unable to take her in for her usual six month stay. Thankfully, my husband was open to the arrangement, and generously accepted the decision without any hesitation, as Grandma settled in our home instead for several months. It was a fortunate circumstance to be able to take good care of her, while enjoying her company for a concentrated period.

The fruit that resulted from four positive grandparent relationships are gifts that can never be taken away.

"Nobody can do for little children what grandparents do. Grandparents sort of sprinkle stardust over the lives of little children."
– Alex Haley –

7

RN Mentors

D uring high school, career aspirations vacillated between elementary education and nursing, eventually settling on a RN diploma program right after graduation. Transitioning to dorm life and a taxing nursing curriculum went decently. A lot of that had to do with spending the duration with a dependable and compatible roommate from high school. Struggling through nursing school together laid the groundwork for what would become an enduring close friendship.

Disciplined effort paid off three years later, when passing state boards paved the way for a position in high-risk pediatrics at a renowned hospital. Being a twenty-one year old novice was overwhelming, but fortunately a number of seasoned co-workers took me under their resourceful wings. Had it not been for their steadying guidance, the introduction to nursing could have very easily been rocky and intimidating. Instead, they set the bar quite high, all the while inspiring the confidence needed to learn the ropes of a demanding occupation. Not always the case for new nurses, the generous mentoring afforded out of the gate was a miraculous advantage that promoted a promising tone for a long-term career.

Over time, the waters in a number of other health care venues were tested: adult/pediatric recovery rooms, obstetrics, wellness, CPR instructing, pain management, and home care.

From the outset, nursing proved an interesting and rewarding role, and it wasn't long before being a nurse became a fundamental slice of self-identity.

"I'm not telling you it's going to be easy.
I'm telling you it's going to be worth it."
– Art Williams –

8

Partners for Life

Crossing paths with my future husband midway through nursing school brought some levity. Mike befriended me in the trying months following the death of little brother Glenny, and from that point on we were a couple. He consistently had my back, and proposed after an uninterrupted three years together.

Marriage introduced two very special people; in-laws who treated me like a daughter from the start. Tight-knit extended relatives on both sides readily welcomed us in to their sizable circles. We came from similar backgrounds, and neither family tried to *undermine* our union, but regularly *fostered* it instead. Acceptance, both individually and as a couple, contributed considerably to the marriage foundation, giving it greater odds of succeeding.

By age twenty-nine, raising a toddler and newborn was in full swing. It helped working as a nurse for a year on a maternity ward prior to delivering our firstborn. With both children, there was a resumption of hospital employment after standard abbreviated six-week leaves, although thoughts of being a stay-at-home mom enticed.

Choices always come with pros and cons, but owning a decision and making the best of it made more sense than wasting energy worrying about what other mothers were doing. Fortunately, a portion of child rearing years were spent working part time, which created a nice balance. Juggling a job and home proved nerve-wracking at times, but Mike was an exceptionally involved father who did his share without additional cajoling required.

Utilizing a team approach and united front helped things from going completely askew, although meals weren't fancy, and house cleaning routines were frequently slipshod or overlooked. The years were hectic as school commitments and sporting events replaced diaper bags and toddler toys. Oftentimes, we were going in completely different directions, working opposite shifts to cover child care needs. Maintaining a third shift nursing job for many years generated chronic sleep deprivation, though it was a decent option that seemed to work at the time.

It was hard to comprehend where the years went, because in what felt like fast-forward mode, our kids morphed into high school graduates embarking on their futures. Before too long, our family expanded with a first grandbaby and wonderful son-in-law.

Grandparenting introduced a whole new dimension of contentment, purpose, and optimistic expectations. It was a second chance to experience childhood milestones, those perhaps not fully appreciated the first time around while in the hub of demanding parenthood. Our Grandma and Grandpa roles were icing on the cake after enjoying twenty-four years of married life.

"A great marriage is not when the 'perfect couple' comes together. It is when an imperfect couple learns to enjoy their differences."
– Dave Meurer –

9

Mom's Passing

For the first thirty-three years of life, the love and guidance of my mother was a profound gift. She was a high-quality woman who was well respected. Her aptitude for prioritizing and handling situations without complaining set a far-reaching example. In light of that tenacious spirit, it was quite a shock when news of a malignant brain tumor shattered the start of her much-anticipated early retirement. It is hard to imagine the thoughts she must have been dealing with when blindsided with such a horrifying discovery.

My adult siblings and I pitched in to help our dad care for her at home. Helplessly watching her health condition rapidly decline was heartbreaking. Assisting with bathing, meal preparation, housekeeping, and doctors' appointments offered sparse slices of steadying order in an otherwise out-of-control and devastating situation. Cancer is no respecter of persons, as it penetrates lives and wreaks havoc.

Mom worked as an RN in the cardiac field for the majority of her lengthy career, and after retirement abruptly found herself in a cancer patient position. She courageously participated in her prescribed treatment plan, but a mere four months later succumbed to the ruinous disease at just fifty-nine years old. Any departing insight and words of wisdom she may have surmised while reflecting on her life would have proved a valuable resource, but such a personal dialogue was never initiated by either of us.

Although she left us far too soon, the dash between her birth date and day of passing had been full of life and love.

*"There's no way to be a perfect mother and
a million ways to be a good one."*
– Jill Churchill –

10

Life-extending Miracles

A local bone marrow drive was held during mom's four month medical nightmare. Publicity for the event caught my attention, even though a donor could not possibly remedy her particular cancer situation. Other desperate people did need marrow, and the screening process seemed simple enough, so getting on board with the program and offering a small blood sample was an easy decision. Donating the same day were my husband, sister, and brother-in-law.

Six years later, the marrow registry called me with information about a possible match. A week of extensive testing verified that the six year old leukemic patient was in fact a viable match: the proverbial needle in a haystack!

The marrow donation was initially successful, but within a year a stem cell donation was also requested. It was done via a different extraction method, and it first required a short course of injections to stimulate my marrow and increase the number of stem cells. Cells being taken *from me* was fine, but there was a wariness about the necessary shots of unfamiliar medication. My apprehension was dealt with, the shots were given, and the stem cell donation with an overnight hospital stay went smoothly.

The little boy and I regularly corresponded through a third party, and his artwork and letters were very sweet. He had gotten stronger, returned to school, and had become a big brother when his sibling was born. On my end, thoughts about trying to meet him and his family after the obligatory three year waiting period was over were entertained. However, his country changed *their* policy within that time frame, so our identities would have to remain anonymous to each other indefinitely. Efforts to see if our marrow match relationship could be grandfathered in under the three-year wait rule, the one actually in place the date of the donation, proved in vain. The chance to meet him could never take place, which was a big disappointment.

A few of his handmade crafts are displayed in our home, and five crystal ornaments from his family hang on the tree every Christmas. Many years went by after the donation when I learned the sad news that he had indeed passed away.

Direct involvement with such an inspiring case was a high point in life; my gift of good health converted into a gift of additional time for someone in desperate need. It was an amazing privilege to pay it forward, all the while being supported by a caring and professional medical transplant team. Despair and frustration over mom's bleak cancer situation triggered joining the marrow registry in the first place, yet the positive ripple effect resulting from that one simple decision to get involved led to a miracle... *and what a front row seat it was!*

Four years later, there was direct involvement with yet another miracle. It happened when the skills acquired working as a CPR instructor for eleven years were put to the test out in the community. It was surreal performing learned techniques on an actual compromised person, instead of an instructional mannequin. The victim and I were both being watched over by a guardian angel, because everything that needed to take place to facilitate a positive outcome materialized. The cardiac arrest was witnessed, the environment was safe, two additional bystanders were present, emergency squad personnel were prompt and professional, and the victim had a favorable outcome, enjoying nearly ten additional years on this earth to love and be loved by many. Every single aspect of a potentially complicated emergency scenario was providentially overseen.

*"You have to see the miracles for
there to be miracles."*
– Jandy Nelson –

Darlene Harting

11

Dad Joins Mom and Glenny

Nine years after mom lost her cancer battle, dad passed away from the cumulative effects of several chronic health issues. The years without mom were difficult, and dad and I got much closer during that period. He did remarry many years after mom passed, buoyed by the companionship of a good woman, and the warm camaraderie of her family and friends.

Seeing his hospital room filled to capacity the day his earthly stay ended brought comfort; *the fruit from a life well-lived clearly visible.* He had been a wonderful dad, and had fostered many relationships throughout his life. Thankfully, he was conscious when surrounded by a large gathering who loved him, so he could take it all in during his final departing hours.

Grieving his loss, there was still peace that came with knowing that Dad, Mom, and Glenny were together.

It was confusing and sad when the second parent, the remaining centering figure for myself and five adult siblings, was no longer there.

"My father didn't tell me how to live;
he lived, and let me watch him do it."
– Clarence Budington Kelland –

Darlene Harting

12

The Circle of Life

A stark finality lingered once both parents and all four grandparents were deceased and physically gone forever; the circle of life a crude obtrusive reality. However, each and every one of them had been an exceptional and influential role model, and their positive imprints would live on.

The scope of God's provision and the far-reaching ramifications of stable roots became increasingly obvious with the passage of time. Their sound legacies remained ever-present sources of inspiration and direction.

As they passed on, newly born nieces, nephews, and grandchildren were welcomed one by one, as future family generations swelled with new life.

"Time goes, you say? Ah, no
alas, time stays, we go."
– Henry Austin Dobson –

Darlene Harting

13

Smooth Sailing

L ife marched on at a brisk and fairly predictable pace and pattern. The years flew by while attending to loved ones and responsibilities; ongoing busyness oftentimes the focus. It *was* possible to become desensitized to a steady diet of goodness and stability; in much the same way that there can be levels of numbness to areas of struggle or iniquity.

I inadvertently lost a degree of conscious appreciation for a relatively uncomplicated life day after day, week after week, and year after year. *The unmerited steadiness that generously came along was appreciated, yet without necessarily acknowledging it was God-given and over-the-top.*

There came a point where smooth sailing was *the expectation*, because thus far that had been my reality. Five fairly unencumbered decades swiftly passed, and the significant fiftieth birthday milestone was reached in a physically and mentally intact state.

Unbeknownst to anyone, a brewing tempest lurked right around the corner; a free fall off the well-situated mountain perch was just weeks away.

"Enjoy the little things, for one day you'll look back and realize they were the big things."
– Robert Brault –

Darlene Harting

PART II

FREE FALLING

Darlene Harting

14

May 1, 2009 — A Deer in Headlights

There was no forewarning of the despair that would prevail before the day was over. It certainly started out quite normally; with a determined 'to do' list and sketchy agenda in mind. A routine eye exam was scheduled for late morning, leaving ample time for a crack of dawn gym session. A first attempt at completing a marathon distance was six months away; an ambitious bucket list goal to commemorate turning fifty. Six half-marathons and four sprint triathlons had already been realized, so planning a 26.2 miler to specifically honor a lifetime of favorable health seemed a doable and tangible way to celebrate the milestone. There were no delusions of running a major portion, but merely an aspiration to cross the finish line in one piece. Training had been progressing decently for several weeks, and the morning felt upbeat after cranking out ten treadmill miles. Life had a pleasant predictable flow for quite some time, and *all was well.*

At the last minute, Mike tagged along to the eye appointment, which was very unusual, but his motive was to snag a walk-in one for himself. Scheduling a check-up to coincide with the first day of the new calendar year for our insurance plan had been intentional on my part. Growing concern was prodding me to notify the optometrist of an eye issue; one not yet mentioned to anyone. Intricate colorful designs had momentarily appeared when my eyes closed for sleep a couple times over the previous two months.

Efforts to accurately describe them to the doctor were topped off with naively optimistic inquiries of whether they could just be caused by eyestrain or aging. It was obviously a suspect manifestation, because with awkward haste he excused himself and contacted a local retinal practice that agreed to evaluate me *within the hour*.

It felt strange when arriving at the unfamiliar office and waiting room dotted with elderly people donning oversized sunglasses. Generally, I had energy to spare and felt youthful, and turning the big 5-0 a month before was already old news. The current development was the first time an eye issue of any kind ever materialized. A thorough history was conducted and eye film results were clearly abnormal, which initiated a phone consult with yet another specialist who wanted to conduct an immediate assessment as well.

The situation was deteriorating visit by visit. A suffocating sense of urgency was closing in as Mike stoically shuttled us to a third appointment in the span of mere hours. He almost never accompanied me on routine doctor visits, nor had he even been privy to the weird eye symptom. Normally I'd be alone, yet there he was right by my side considerately navigating the downward spiral.

The concluding doctor confirmed a critical finding that blindsided us. With professionalism and authentic sensitivity, he broke the news of a medium to large-sized melanoma mass inside one eye. It was the first time I had ever even heard of that type of cancer penetrating the eye. The ignorance was completely irrelevant, because diagnostic images highlighted a significant flaw that could not be denied, and other specifics about the abnormal area crudely sealed the deal. Available treatment options and the unknown cause and rarity of the condition were patiently explained.

The absurdity of being afflicted with something so rare was disorienting and difficult to fathom. But well-rehearsed nursing instincts kicked in; the need to understand what was happening in order to make informed decisions. Numb, yet at the same time struggling to listen to dark unwanted facts: *a reluctant spectator watching my unproblematic life do a one-eighty.*

By all accounts the day's onset was unremarkable, yet only hours later the mutation from a healthy middle-aged woman to a panic-stricken cancer statistic was real and horrifying. Up until then, alarming medical stories were only heard through the grapevine...*always about other people.*

Barely any words were uttered on the surreal drive home: the precipitous news an uninvited elephant stuffed in our compact car.

> **"A sudden, bold, and unexpected question doth**
> **many times surprise a man and lay him open."**
> **– Francis Bacon –**

Darlene Harting

15

Preventative Healthcare

The unexpected diagnosis instigated a distress unlike any experienced thus far in life. Sorting through the abrupt deviation from long-standing equilibrium was intimidating; the pronounced unrest a foreign state of mind.

An element of surprise insistently smoldered. A thirty year medical background *should have* prompted an immediate evaluation of the colorful patterns the very first time they appeared.

Some medical conditions are particularly time-sensitive, where a sense of urgency is paramount in order for interventions to be done within the allotted time frames necessary for optimal outcomes. For example, with strokes and heart attacks the window is very small, and the need to seek immediate medical assistance is *critical* in reducing mortality and morbidity. Had I already missed the boat for timely effective treatment of this eye affliction?

The bottom line was that the colorful patterns were blatant, yet the warning not readily heeded. Discounting them defied logic; normally being someone attuned to bodily changes and promptly checking out unusual indicators. Procrastinating about the occasional bright eye designs had been a poor decision, and it was not easy taking ownership of my sluggish response.

Preventative health measures made provable sense for a long time. Working a side job as a wellness nurse for over a decade had been advantageous, because of the inherent accountability to practice what was being preached to clients. Incorporating consistent exercise and better eating patterns in my mid-forties yielded a decent weight loss and ensuing health benefits. The goal was to proactively enhance the baseline prior to heading even further down the unavoidable aging path. Cigarettes, excessive alcohol, and recreational drugs would have compromised desired longevity, and dodging them was easy enough. In essence, it felt hypocritical and unfair to counsel others on the preemptive practices *they* should be doing, without at least attempting to apply the same suggestions. Maintaining the irreplaceable gift of an unencumbered and able body was a priority. None of the well-intentioned efforts to forestall illness seemed to matter one damn bit at the moment, because cancer still managed to rear its heinous intrusive head.

Ironically, there was conscientiousness about watching for skin melanoma. A family member's bout of skin cancer, coupled with my own light complexion, was enough cause to seek regular skin inspections with a trusted dermatologist. The intimate nature of an annual full body examination was routinely awkward, but necessary, so any embarrassment had to be deliberately blocked out. It was certainly preferable to struggling later on with the belated discovery of an *advanced lesion,* one that may have been caught in an earlier more treatable stage had it not been for squeamish self-consciousness. Peace of mind came with every annual nonthreatening skin appraisal. Early detection made perfect sense, due to a heightened regard for melanoma's gravity.

"Good health is not something we can buy. However, it can be an extremely valuable savings account."
– Anne Wilson Schaef –

Darlene Harting

16

Twice Spared

An upper back lesion was discovered and biopsied several months earlier, with the initial pathology report yielding an irregular and non-reassuring finding. Fortunately, a second more extensive review established that the suspect area was not cancerous.

A few years before that scare, a disturbing possibility of breast cancer ominously hovered when a routine annual mammogram detected a questionable area. There was a 50-50 chance the results could be unfavorable *that time* as well, but a determining biopsy disproved any malignancy.

Optimal health had already been spared twice in the past, but the eye mass's distinctly menacing tone taunted that second chances had come to an abrupt unforeseen end. Far too many friends and relatives never got their second chance, so how was it even possible to encounter yet another rescue, when two potentially threatening conditions had already been miraculously cancelled out?

"How quickly we forget God's great deliverances in our lives. How easily we take for granted the miracles He performed in our past."
– David Wilkerson –

Darlene Harting

17

An Introspective Night

L ittle sleep came the first night, as random clips flooded consciousness and competed for attention. A multitude of pluses came to light, and enveloped with an acute impressiveness of all that had been bestowed in life. Seemingly, the cancer alert roused a wide ranging review of past and present endowments. Nonetheless, admiration of the pleasing even-keeled momentum had dulled over time, and the sheer magnitude of overflowing blessings had inadvertently become commonplace.

A heightened self-awareness yielded satisfaction and pride about various behaviors, and discontent about others. Denial about the diagnosis was being bypassed, going directly to bargaining in the grieving process: aspiring to be more fearless, mindful, and appreciative, and praying for a lifeline extension to be able to have the opportunity to try.

Regrets alternately conflicted with affirmative recollections while scrutinizing past choices, behaviors, priorities, and omissions. It was a baffling concept that life might be coming to an end *far sooner than ever imagined.* Which aspects of overall spirit and conduct in life would linger if I were no longer here?

Darlene Harting

"Life can only be understood backwards;
but it must be lived forwards."
– Soren Kierkegaard –

18

Validation of a Gem

An odd discernible urging to address some dismissive spousal behaviors came out of nowhere the night of diagnosis, and in the darkness apologies were made to Mike for my intermittent hurried and detached attitude. Multitasking and focusing on everything that needed to *get done* oftentimes resulted in a rushed and disconnected mindset. Even so, any inattentiveness on my end never deterred him from verbally affirming his regard *for me* on a frequent basis. Without fail, he had been 'all in' with everything in our married life. The physically demanding construction work he did for years to support the family undoubtedly took a toll on his body, and he was also a very actively involved father to our children. Not only was he an ongoing gift of a partner, but specifically a partner who was consistently checked in. Yet, somehow over time that had begun to be taken for granted to some degree.

Witnessing umpteen couples set-apart by death or divorce regularly emphasized just how quickly relationships *can* shift. Even so, having grown used to having a committed spouse after more than two decades together fostered a naïve and contented assumption that nothing *would ever change between us.* Angst about the day's alarming medical disclosure prompted a look back on just how much we had been through together, highlighted rewarding aspects of our integrated lives, reminded me how safe and loved he always made me feel, and what an exceptional man and life partner Mike was.

"The more often we see the things around us –
even the beautiful and wonderful things – the
more they become invisible to us. That is why we
often take for granted the beauty of this world:
the flowers, the trees, the birds, the clouds – even
those we love. Because we see things so often, we
see them less and less."
– Joseph B. Wirthlin –

19

A Glaring Truth is Finally Faced

Reminiscing continued, bringing raw emotions to the surface while sifting through memories of my regular deficient outlay of attention toward my dog Sugar. Flashbacks of willful and prolonged oblivion toward her could no longer be overlooked. Working third shift for most of her life resulted in varying levels of chronic sleep deprivation. Insufficient sleep was definitely a contributing factor, *but absolutely no excuse*, for a standard impatience with her. My attitude needed a major adjustment for quite some time, yet little adjusting was ever done. Fortunately, she got loads of attention and affection from Mike and the kids. She was a good girl that deserved TLC, but my scanty contribution had been substandard tolerance.

There was no way to go back and undo years of emotional indifference, the damage was done and an innocent dog had paid the price. The sharp unannounced review of the long-term callous attitude hit like a ton of bricks, convicting and finally appalling me. While crying on and off about it all night, the glaring truth was faced.

Ignoring an imbalance in a personal relationship could bring regrets too, perhaps when the status of one of the involved parties changes or deteriorates. The current remorse stemmed from a pattern of inconsiderate conduct knowingly perpetrated with a pet. It may have been an unusual concern to be gripped by when initially blindsided by cancer, but there it was right smack in the forefront of thoughts. Being cognizant of the stingy behavior, but obstinately opting not to improve was so wrong.

Depending on the staging of the new cancer diagnosis, the window of opportunity to amend Sugar's care might be closing sooner than later, *and only then* was the frigid attitude truly seen for what it had been all along: a sinful omission and selfish stupid waste.

> *"The truth doesn't hurt*
> *unless it ought to."*
> *– B.C. Forbes –*

20

Settle Down....Look Around

Busyness had inadvertently been a spirit sapper. There were limited opportunities to process input before preparing for the next wave of bills, groceries, appointments, chores, work shifts, social commitments, and random responsibilities. Technology bragged of making things easier, steering transactions online all the time, yet I stubbornly preferred to talk to a live person on the phone when dealing with any business concerns, go to brick and mortar stores and banks, and pay bills through the mail: a crotchety stubborn dinosaur not always wanting to change with the times.

My perhaps skewed perception was that many functions were actually getting *more complicated*, oftentimes leaving a residual low level frustration. Mike sporadically saying, "Laugh, smile, *life is good*!" came to mind. The clarity of his periodic decree resonated in the dark; my biography *had been* uncomplicated, physically healthy, mentally well-grounded, and meaningful. It seemed undue concern was being placed on completing tasks, and not enough on smelling, and at times even noticing, fragrant roses in full bloom along the way. It was somehow possible to remain completely functional, while unthinkingly plodding through agendas and going through the motions on any number of given days. The intermittent robotic trajectory clouded recognition of an extraordinary life.

Darlene Harting

"In all the chaos and hurry, do not forget to notice the beauty and miracle of this world. Slow down. Notice. Observe. Be aware. Allow presence and awe to come back into your life."
– Brendon Burchard –

21

Not Alone

Some semblance of peace came with knowing God was with me, and that in spite of multiple shortcomings, general conduct in life had been based on respect for myself and others. The *life is short* reference was hitting way too close to home though.

Had a decent portion of the God-given potential for which I was created been utilized? I grieved the cumulative passing of time; *nonrefundable time that had often gone unheeded.*

"O Lord, you have examined my heart
and know everything about me."
– Psalm 139:1 NLT –

Darlene Harting

22

Morning Confirmed Reality

Unwanted reality instantly bombarded the senses upon awakening. Mike and I spent a short time sorting out the situation with our grown children. There was one point when my tears flowed, and my grandson unhesitatingly tried comforting with a kiss and hug. He was only two and a half years old, yet clearly empathetic. The tender rudimentary expressions of concern meant the world to his distraught Grandma.

Regretful stewing continued in earnest concerning dismissal of the visual disturbances experienced for several weeks prior to diagnosis. Would the outcome have been different if a doctor had been consulted the very first time it happened? The mass may have been brewing for many years before the indicative signs ever presented, thus making a two month delay insignificant. Yes, the response had definitely been tardy, but a lesson had been learned, and it was important to let it go. Unnecessarily dwelling on it would not be productive or change the outcome, but it sure did not make sense that things could go wrong *so quickly.*

It was a Saturday, and going to church the following morning was considered, although my attendance had fluctuated and become rather unpredictable for many years. Participating would usually resume at some point, then gradually other commitments would take precedence and start replacing church services. Attention was directed toward putting all the ducks in a row in terms of family, employment, finances, hobbies......you name it. Concentration was focused on orchestrating a lengthy and uncomplicated future, yet only a meager investment had been allotted for spiritual discernment and maturation. I *knew about* God from a young age, and never doubted His all-encompassing love, but diligence towards getting to *know Him more* vacillated.

A plea for physical healing was *why* making time to attend church was suddenly a priority, arousing sentiments of guilt and fraudulence. In spite of well-meaning loved ones, the new medical burden yielded an acute sense of being completely alone. Was I prepared to meet my Maker?

"Adversity is like a strong wind. It tears away
from us all but the things that cannot be torn,
so that we see ourselves as we really are."
– Arthur Golden –

23

Seeking Answers

Morning announced itself with the sweet sound of a jabbering grandson; his presence a beacon in the uncertain fog.

Mike and I talked briefly with the Pastor upon our arrival at the church service. Acquaintance with him spanned over two decades, having lost touch in more recent years, and we filled him in on what had transpired the previous days.

At the end of the service, he appealed to church members for intercessory prayers, specifically asking for the *healing of deepest need*. Physical healing was my hope, yet he seemed to refer to something more. The congregation had a warm welcoming vibe, and the service was thought-provoking. Messages came through loud and clear, and appeased in spite of my oppressive panic.

A few family members and friends stopped by the house later in the day, and interactions had a fresh palpable richness to them *more obvious than ever before*. The current trepidation highlighted the considerable support systems richly infusing life all along.

An unexpected Sunday phone call came from the doctor who made the definitive diagnosis. He was leaving the state to attend a conference and called to check up before leaving. What kind of doctor does that? It seemed highly unusual, and the earnest attempt to share personal concern was touching.

His considerate inquiry left no doubt the medical ordeal had been placed in special hands.

Before long, another day came to an end. Mike was a rock, holding nothing back in his genuine efforts to console. His comforting gestures were especially apparent during the night hours, when apprehension escalated.

"We have to pray with our eyes on God, not on the difficulties."
– Oswald Chambers –

24

Focus on the Present

A wakening, I scanned the bedroom while covering the right eye. There was a novel appreciation for having good eyesight, present since birth, yet just accepted without even thinking. Once a portion of that sight was going to be taken away is when the gift of unencumbered vision was fully realized: *We don't know what we've got until it's gone* no longer simply a cliché.

Different treatment options had been presented, based on the size and location of the mass. With minimal personal indecision, enucleation (removal of the affected eye) was selected. It was reassuring to learn that although it *can* happen, the malady does not usually affect both eyes. Surgical eradication was only days away, and the punctual scheduling to remove the detrimental cluster of cells brought both trepidation *and* relief. The sooner the mass was gone, the better.

A girlfriend passed along the phone number of a local man who had the same diagnosis and treatment a few years prior. A call was initiated, and he and his wife patiently shared a helpful description of his surgery and full recovery over the phone. They never even met me, yet they unselfishly made themselves available, and took the time to inform and encourage. Their personable outreach resulted in a measurable calming down about the upcoming surgery and aftercare.

Mike and I were paid a visit when friends made through our son's high school wrestling career offered to stop by and pray together. We were surprised when six of them exited the van in the driveway. The notion they all spontaneously took time in the middle of their days to extend themselves meant a lot. The uncertain path ahead sure seemed laden with well-intentioned people.

A wallet sized poem card was left behind about finding God in the present moments, not in regrets of the past, or fears about the future. The need for, and timing of the message, was so perfect it startled.

Unnecessarily overthinking past choices and priorities was causing a degree of angst.

Concerns about the future, and worrying about the uncertainties of it was only compounding anxiety. It was a vicious cycle gaining momentum one fear at a time.

In order to regain a foothold, attention had to be redirected toward the present, and the diverse ways God was reaching out.

Fretting and wallowing in worry without restraint for days had led nowhere, and reading one lucid poem helped clarify that truth. Was it really *a coincidence* that the poem's subject matter precisely mirrored internal conflicts?

A friend stopped by in the evening bringing along her pastor and his wife. The fact that they barely knew me did not hold this generous couple back from offering their encouragement. It was a thoughtful gesture, and their obvious confidence in the power of intercessory prayer was the second witness in one day. My own prayer life had taken a back seat for quite some time, so it was especially humbling to hear such heartfelt petitions verbalized by others on my behalf.

Another busy and emotional day ended with the simple bedtime ritual adopted when my grandson was a baby. Our routine seemed especially precious in light of the looming unknown. Would the coveted role of Grandma be winding down and coming to an end in the near future? Extra songs and stories were added to our usual repertoire, trying to prolong the gratifying sensation of his sweet closeness.

In the past, song lyrics from assorted genres would sometimes have a way of driving home different messages. A given song can be the perfect vehicle to get a point across. Christian music CDs were dropped off during the week by family; the songs offering safe, yet challenging, points of view. Playing softly through earphones, they served as a major source of overnight influence; when confusion about the current situation kicked into high gear.

"This is my command- be strong and courageous!
Do not be afraid or discouraged. For the LORD
your God is with you wherever you go."
– Joshua 1:9 NLT –

Darlene Harting

25

Had the Cancer Spread?

Tests were scheduled for later in the day to determine if the eye cancer had already invaded elsewhere. Unfortunately, systematically spreading itself around is something cancer does *very well.* There was no way of knowing how long the mass had actually been growing. It bordered on being labeled large, so it was feasible cells could have escaped the confinement of the eye area.

Like clockwork, Mike was present at the hospital for the tests. He just happened to be off between construction jobs, and awaiting notification to return to work. Periodic layoffs had been the norm throughout our marriage. It was all dependent on when a job ended, when new ones would start, as well as the weather and other variables. Usually I tolerated the work irregularities decently, but annoyance and testiness inevitably set in with extended layoffs. There was probably some repressed jealousy, because the possibility of a suspended work situation in the nursing field was so remote. Why couldn't for just once a layoff be the only option for a substantial (but limited) period of time; a welcome respite from demanding hospital work?

It is so true about being careful what we wish for, because going to work as usual would be perfect, and far superior to the current mess. The long-coveted reprieve from work demands finally came, but at a very high cost.

A technician seemed especially kind while administering an ordered procedure, and other compassionate people materialized at every turn. It was during common interactions that God could be seen working *through individuals.* His presence was extensive and impressive, when a conscious effort to notice was made.

Two lingering days would have to pass before any diagnostic results would be interpreted and available, but efforts aimed to distract from obsessing about them were in vain.

Advice to live each day as if it were our last, and the truth that no one knows when our time on earth will be up are well known principles, yet rarely personally considered. Inadvertently losing sight of the certainty of mortality, and fabricating a false sense of security and control over circumstances was my modus operandi.

A usual determined spirit was fading. An optimist at heart, I pretty much believed there's some type of solution to every obstacle, and approached situations by changing to Plan B if Plan A no longer worked adequately. If Plan B no longer fit the bill, investigating a potential Plan C would take place before making a calculated change. The reference is mainly to employment situations, but the approach has worked well in most arenas. It always made more sense to modify, or get out of a situation, instead of simply carrying on and sticking with Plan A when it no longer worked, and just powerlessly complaining. Nevertheless, the surprising cancer alert reeked of pessimism, while obliterating positivity.

The unpredictability of life reverberated, and a few people with resolute faith that resembled a shield came to mind. No matter what life bombards with, they remain grounded. It was obvious that getting through the shaky stretch at hand was going to require faith and trust.

Retiring for the night, a longing for life's prior evenness enveloped.

"Teach us to realize the brevity of life,
so that we may grow in wisdom."
– Psalm 90:12 NLT –

Darlene Harting

26

A Rich Woman

The mailman commented on the heavy volume of cards cramming our mailbox. Get-well messages poured in from co-workers not seen since my resignation from a maternity nursing department four years prior. Friendships fostered during that twenty-one year employment chapter surfaced, with many caring thoughts expressed. Current co-workers supportively rallied as well. As if that wasn't more than enough, there was a steady flow of goodwill from family and friends.

It's a Wonderful Life is a favorite movie. The fictional tale tells of George Bailey, a good man experiencing a financial catastrophe so overwhelming to him that he sees suicide and the payout of a life insurance policy to his wife and children as the only solution. An angel, Clarence, comes to show him what life would have been like had he never been born. My favorite scenes come at the end of the movie, when all the friends George made during his lifetime mobilize and rally to his aid in his time of need. He discovers he is the richest man in his close knit town, because of a multitude of meaningful relationships. The fundamental messages and poignant closing portrayal always a tear-jerker.

Reflecting on a generous number of meaningful relationships yielded a deeper appreciation of what *an incredibly rich woman I was* because of them. The extent of personal wealth was becoming increasingly obvious, just as it had for George Bailey.

"To be rich in friends is
to be poor in nothing."
– Lilian Whiting –

27

The Best Possible News!

Feeling both hopefulness and dread, the day arrived to find out if any further cancer had been detected.

If the news was unfavorable, there was a key piece of information better left unsaid as Mike and I entered the doctor's office. The doctor was asked not to divulge any time-sensitive longevity predictions if metastatic sites had been discovered. After all, my brother Glenny had almost reached his eighth birthday, even though specialists had estimated a numbing two-year life expectancy. More peace would be had by putting today's results and any specific projections in God's hands.

Smiling broadly, the doctor updated us that nothing abnormal had been detected in specifically tested sites. It was the best possible news: the level of protection was a miracle!

Totally amazed, we floated out of the office on cloud nine. Excited calls were made to family and friends, and a celebratory dinner with our children and grandson topped off the surreal evening. The imminent surgical eye removal the following morning was eclipsed by the pacifying summary that the injurious cancer had stayed safely contained: a clean bill of health!

Mentally exhausted, yet lulled by the confident report, sleep came swiftly for the first night since diagnosis a week prior.

"From the bitterness of disease man
learns the sweetness of health."
– Catalan Proverb –

28

A Successful Surgical Intervention

R eady or not…surgery day arrived. Each staff member who rendered care did so with professionalism *and kindness*. The anesthesiologist referred to the "boss upstairs" really being the one in control: so true. Once anesthesia wore off, the surgeon assured there had been no complications.

Settling in the recovery area where we would be spending the night, Mike and I savored the official cancer-free status. There was minimal post-operative discomfort, but it sure felt strange knowing there was no longer an eye under the bulky bandage.

A mere eight days had passed since the abrupt diagnosis, yet it proved to be a defining and enlightening interruption. A subtle inkling to eventually write about the fleeting persuasive period took hold during the quiet pensive recovery hours.

Knowing things could have turned out *so much worse* than they actually had was such a relief. Losing an eye might be the extent of the damage, and end of the road for this medical nightmare. If so, a miracle of escaping *utterly unscathed* had taken place.

The morning brought bright sunshine and a hospital discharge…..things were looking up!

"Be happy for this moment. This moment is your life."
– Omar Khayyam –

Darlene Harting

PART III

HINDSIGHT
IS
20/20

Darlene Harting

29

Worrying was Bondage

The exciting pre-op report that the lesion had not metastasized *should have* been ample assurance of a clean bill of health, but that was not the case. Of course there was rational understanding the cancer was surgically eliminated, but emotional recovery lagged behind.

Doctors and test results indicated the malignancy was gone, so not being able to fully believe it seemed ridiculous. The combination of my baseline questioning predisposition and lengthy nursing background contributed to an inclination to try to protect personal medical interests, just in case. A bit of a skeptic at times, and still somewhat shaken about abruptly finding a mass in the first place, it was a stretch wrapping my head around the news things might actually be fine after all.

The bondage of worry lingered, and having any doubts that God's wonderful provision and plan were real brought on guilt as well. The peace of mind that should have been there was obscured by dense uneasiness.

One specific additional diagnostic test was mentioned (in fine print only) on one report, suggesting a more definitive clarification of an area. Happening to notice the suggestion, I dwelled on it, could not ignore it, and basically it became an obsession to make sure that extra test *was* done. The anxiety was self-induced, nevertheless, the foreboding that something potentially fixable was going to be missed if the specific test was not done could not be dismissed. I had agitated enough irrational concern that there was a lesion somewhere; it just had not been found yet. Hypothetical scenarios of returning for a six-month check-up, only to learn a calamitous cluster of cells had somehow escaped detection and now it was too late, preoccupied thoughts. Eventually the additional test was done, and the favorable results helped subdue anxiety.

Worrying served no purpose, all it did was block contentment and waste energy. It's hard to understand why I clung to it so tightly.

Thankfully, after a number of healthy six-month check-ups, the sequential evidences of wellness were difficult to dispute. Finally, the idea that things really were going to be okay was comprehended.

That being said...the limitation to one area was a remarkable miracle.

"Worry does not empty tomorrow of its sorrow;
It empties today of its strength."
– Corrie ten Boom –

30

Potential Influence

With over half of a lifetime spent as a healthcare provider, I was out of my element in the less familiar recipient role.

While a patient getting ordered tests and pre-op/post-op surgical care, even simple positive gestures from staff were noticed. Heightened anxiety induced a sharper appreciation of even the subtlest efforts. Staff introducing themselves using eye contact, clarifying instructions, and showing some degree of empathy all went a long way. These deeds are not hard to do, and should be the norm in service roles, but unfortunately they are not always done. Shifts can get so busy and workloads very taxing, but when simple gestures such as these get overlooked it is unfair to patients and their families.

The nursing occupation yielded exposure to quite varied employment settings over the years. Being caught in a cancer *patient* role for even just a flash triggered thoughts about my own nurse demeanor in the past while rendering care.

Working in home care acquainted me with young and medically challenged patients whose families selflessly managed their care 24/7. Seeing the various ways ongoing hurdles were dealt with was inspirational. Hopefully, my being in the loop helped to lessen the load while a nurse on a number of special long-term home care cases.

My longest employment stint, and best fit, was in obstetrics. There were ample opportunities to be with new moms and dads when they were vulnerable, all the while striving to be an asset for them during pivotal hospital experiences. Goals were to provide safe care to mothers and babies, and to empower parents with confidence before discharging them home. Nevertheless, the weightiness of disposition and interacting style while rendering care was not fully grasped *at the time*. Shifts were busy and patient assignments often substantial, so prioritizing and getting everything done correctly in the allotted time frame was an understandable mindset.

The inherent responsibility to be a nurturing influence was realized more fully in hindsight, while looking back on the lengthy chapter.

Opportunities to be a positive influence, either through words or actions, materialize randomly on a daily basis for everyone. How these possibilities are utilized is what counts.

"Act as if what you do makes
a difference. It does."
– William James –

31

Grandma's Angel

*G*randma's Angel was the nickname given to my first grandson throughout his three week stay of my diagnosis and surgery. My daughter immediately cleared her schedule, and left her home with son in tow to stay at our house to be a supportive presence. Her little guy was an effective diversion during the challenging period: his innocence, enthusiasm, and boundless energy were better than any medicine.

Though just a toddler, he conveyed sweet rudimentary displays of empathy, because this quality had been consistently demonstrated *to him* since birth. His childish caring mannerisms mirrored all the love his parents and extended family had shown him during his short life. It was a pleasure watching my daughter blossom into an endearing mom.

Children can be lifted up by even simple nurturing gestures from parents, grandparents, extended family, doctors, teachers, coaches, and others with whom they have contact. The invested positivity can then be paid forward.

In the blink of an eye children grow to young adults entering society, and they need to be well equipped to extend love to others as they make their way in the world.

"It is easier to build strong children than to repair broken men."
– Frederick Douglass –

Darlene Harting

32

Too Little…..Too Late

As previously noted, ownership and shame over omissions with Sugar hit with full force the panicky night following cancer disclosure. Perhaps thoughts that life might be ending in the near future overwhelmed, triggering the abrupt scrutiny of a behavior allowed to go on far too long. The regret-laden admission had hung heavily over those initial night hours. In any case, an immediate resolve to do better set in, with much improved behaviors starting the following morning. As time went on, the betterment effortlessly continued. Generously showing her affection was so easy, so it was ludicrous that I had not been doing it all along.

Her sweet and loyal spirit seemed *so obvious*, yet that same spirit had consistently been snubbed. Going through the motions without investing my heart in nurturing her heart had been the status quo. Sadly, she died only four short months after experiencing my cleaned up act. Clearly, it was too little….and far too late.

How could anyone be cold to a lovable dog….and why? Getting a dog had not been my idea, nevertheless I had willingly got on board with the plan and looked forward to it. It is possible some buried resentment over ensuing pet responsibilities, combined with chronic insufficient sleep working third shift, contributed to a general impatience with her. Any speculations about *why* are immaterial though, because in the end the indifference was absolutely unacceptable.

After much discussion, and soul-searching on my part, Mike and I welcomed Hoss, a new male puppy, into our home a year and a half after Sugar passed away. Capable of so much more, I knew I could and would, be a fully engaged pet owner this time around. Hoss was a pleasure to be around and an integral part of our family, and the unconditional love in his eyes was ever-apparent.

Some good may hopefully come out of publicly sharing a private wrong. If even a handful of readers can relate to similar negative patterns and nip them in the bud, the disclosure will have been well worth it.

Although I felt convicted when finally owning up to the unsuitable conduct, there was never a sense God condemned me. On the contrary, a desire to do better and be better was instilled. A valuable lesson about omission was learned: not doing the right thing can be as detrimental as doing the wrong thing.

Thankfully, second chances are freely available in any setting.

"Though no one can go back and make a
brand-new start, anyone can start from now
and make a brand-new ending."
– Carl Bard –

33

Vibrant Green Grass

It is human nature to compare ourselves to others at times, and think the grass is surely greener other than where we are, or who we are, at various times. In so doing, there can be oversight of all we *are* actually blessed with. It is pretty difficult to be grateful *and* dissatisfied at the same time. However, simply striving to be satisfied with self and present possessions at any given time is sometimes easier said than done.

It makes sense that if more focus is put on being a better steward and nurturing any gifts I've been given, it would leave a lot less time to concern myself with what I'm not, or what I don't have. In doing that, unnecessary and fruitless comparisons with others could surely be minimized.

Nevertheless, appreciation of the vibrant green grass in life is deepening with both advancing age and varying experiences. Any strengths, faults, personality traits, talents, weaknesses, struggles and surroundings that are creating the tapestry of life are all part of God's plan.

> *"All we have is all we need. All we need is the awareness of how blessed we really are."*
> *– Sarah Ban Breathnach –*

Darlene Harting

34

Make Room for Dreams

The reality of mortality could not be ignored while going through this experience, but it is not something considered on a regular basis. Following attendance at wakes and funerals is usually when mortality views are provoked. Many loved ones' lives have ended far too prematurely.

Mom died at fifty-nine, a mere six months after retiring, and plans for enjoying her golden years with dad vanished. She had worked hard both in and out of the home, raised seven children, and nursed a seriously ill son until his early death. A lengthy relaxing retirement was eagerly anticipated, but it was not to be. Although dad made it to seventy-one, that age still seems quite young, especially in light of its ever-increasing nearness.

While contemplating a potentially poor prognosis and early demise, one realization really stood out. Worrying about trivial things and not stretching enough in the past suddenly seem so silly and wasteful. Why do we shrink or hold ourselves back, when we might not even be here tomorrow? We don't have to be good dancers to dance, great singers to sing, or talented writers to write. Why can't those things be done simply because they are enjoyable pursuits?

People's dreams are likely shelved, put on the back burner, or completely discarded on a frequent basis. Life tends to get in the way, but at the same time *it is short*, so there is nothing to lose in trying to pursue our aspirations.

"Never let the odds keep you from doing what you know in your heart you were meant to do."
– H. Jackson Brown, Jr. –

35

Ahhh…..Moving on

Everything was winding down and moving along. Visual adjustments went quite well, due to a long standing optometrist who worked his magic fine-tuning a lens prescription. The referred occularist making the prosthetic was second to none, and being surrounded by many of his patients' painted glass eyes in various creative stages during office appointments started feeling increasingly normal. It was fascinating that he merely looked at my good eye, *without even taking a picture*, and after several phases the prosthetic was a perfect match.

The wait to obtain the specifics of the melanoma was well worth it, because the determination was there was no need for drug therapy. Complete removal *was* the treatment, and the beginning of an eventual fading out of a disruptive chapter.

Co-workers had unselfishly piled on extended hours in an attempt to provide uninterrupted home care coverage for a patient during my unexpected leave. As a result, a few aspects of the schedule were altered, and not as appealing, upon return to work. The main thing was there was *still* a good job to resume.

Appreciation and contentment in working, running errands, exercising, and even doing mundane chores was deeper than it had previously been. There wasn't much grumbling about responsibilities for quite some time; probably because it felt so great to be doing *anything other than still having cancer.*

Happy to be moving on, the resumption of the unproblematic and familiar pace of life was so very sweet.

"After a storm comes a calm."
– Matthew Henry –

FAST FORWARD TEN YEARS

Reaching the sixtieth milestone birthday in conjunction with the ten year anniversary of a cancer-free status *and* completion of this book marked a triple celebration!

A decade has passed at lightning speed, and it is hard to fathom how quickly the time vanished. Well, the years were certainly full: job changes, children relocating, our son swearing in as a proud new fireman, Mike's retirement, and the births of more beautiful grandchildren. The period had some very sad times as well, with deep voids left due to the passing away of treasured family members, friends, and our dog Hoss.

Measures of personal wealth have increased exponentially, because of scores of valuable relationships gained along the way. The older I get, the more the circle of good people in my life swells..........yet, the smaller the world seems. *Six degrees of separation* is seeming a more plausible concept, as friends, family, co-workers, and acquaintances are randomly intersecting with increasing frequency.

Some lessons *so* vivid during the storm have faded with the passing of time and resumption of an even-keeled momentum. It seems there is an inverse relationship: with an increased sense of stability and independence comes a decreased degree of my leaning on and seeking the Lord. Old habits of distracted busyness are hard to break, and some days it seems I have learned nothing at all and am back to square one. There is infinite room for learning, growing, and gaining wisdom along the way.

Nevertheless, it was very beneficial revisiting the past feelings, regrets, priorities, and lessons that were highlighted during the rocky patch, because never losing sight of them is paramount.

About two years post-cancer, a calling to sing solos at church was sensed. Perhaps sharing some of the same songs that personally uplifted me during the shaky medical period? It was surely an odd concept, since already fifty-two, with no vocal background or past stints in any choirs. Still, baby steps were tentatively taken, and singing both secular and Christian music slowly blossomed into an involved and fulfilling pursuit. Simply being a vehicle and singing pivotal melodies at worship services is when a connection with the Lord really resonates. Being present at services in order to hear and internalize valuable messages is helpful, so the opportunity to sing them along with fellow choir members is a humbling bonus.

Much happiness and multiple music related friendships have been generated through singing, but it all would have been completely bypassed had the baby steps not been taken. It is strange to think of all that would have been missed had the comfort zone in that area been left unstretched. I'm very grateful, random as it was, to have pursued the prompting to try singing, because of the many ways it has served to enrich life.

Having functional physical abilities and sound cognitive and mental faculties at any age is *not a given*. Turning sixty with these things still intact is a blessing not taken for granted. Mike continues to be a rock, watching out for me in all things. I'm grateful to be growing old together, and pray there are many years on the horizon!

"For I know the plans I have for you", says the Lord. "They are plans for good and not for disaster, to give you a future and a hope."
– Jeremiah 29:11 NLT –

ACKNOWLEDGEMENTS

Sincere thanks to all inspirational quote authors that were noted, as well as those who encouraged this account in any way, and to God for planting the vision and sustaining all efforts.

BOOK CLUB QUESTIONS

1. Can you relate to the author's greater sensitivity to God's presence in the uncertainty and fear of the diagnosis than when life had a smooth course? Was there a time in your life when this happened to you, or someone close to you?

2. What are some assets or people in your life that you may have become used to and a bit desensitized to over time?

3. Did you find the summarizing quotes and scriptures at the end of each chapter meaningful? Which ones especially caught your attention and why?

4. What general themes did you find yourself connecting with the most? Were there any themes that you could not personally identify with?

5. Do you think the sting and subsequent lessons learned during critical life events can dull, or even be forgotten, with the passing of time and resumption of balance? Can you recall any personal, national, or international events where you've seen this happen?

6. What are your thoughts, or perhaps personal struggles, with the task-oriented mindset that is mentioned?

7. How has your childhood upbringing influenced the ways you view life and deal with circumstances?

8. Why do you think the author chose to examine and divulge the remorseful feelings stemming from an unengaged

attitude toward her dog? Did someone or something in your life come to mind?

9. What was the main takeaway from this book for you?

10. What do you think were some of the obstacles and reasons why it took ten years for the dream of authoring to come to fruition? Is there a dream or goal that has slipped through your fingers over the years that you hope to revive and complete? What steps can you start taking to make that happen?

Thank you for your support in choosing
Hidden in Plain Sight for your book club.

CPSIA information can be obtained
at www.ICGtesting.com
Printed in the USA
FFHW011131151219
56892291-62544FF